Dad, Grandpa Winter, and a Cow, circa 1938.

Granny Winter and Dad, circa 1935.

Grandpa Winter (left) and a coworker, circa 1939.

David and Dad, with the family dog, circa 1938.

For my father, Rodgers Lee Winter—J.W.

For Jean Stauffer with love—K.B.R.

Text copyright © 2011 by Jonah Winter
Illustrations copyright © 2011 by Kimberly Bulcken Root
All rights reserved. Published in the United States by Schwartz & Wade Books, an imprint of Random House
Children's Books, a division of Random House, Inc., New York.
Schwartz & Wade Books and the colophon are trademarks of Random House, Inc.
Visit us on the Web! www.randomhouse.com/kids
Educators and librarians, for a variety of teaching tools, visit us at www.randomhouse.com/teachers

Library of Congress Cataloging-in-Publication Data
Winter, Jonah. Born and bred in the Great Depression / Jonah Winter ;
illustrated by Kimberly Root.—1st ed.   p. cm.
Summary: A boy remembers his father's stories about life in East Texas during the Great Depression.
ISBN 978-0-375-86197-0 (trade) — ISBN 978-0-375-96197-7 (glb) — ISBN 978-0-375-98385-6 (ebook)
1. Depressions—1929—Texas, East—Juvenile literature. 2. Texas, East—History—20th century—Juvenile
literature. 3. Texas, East—Social conditions—20th century—Juvenile literature. I. Root, Kimberly Bulcken, ill.
II. Title.   F391.W73 2011   976.4'062—dc22   2009048809

The text of this book is set in Tribute.
The illustrations were rendered on Arches 140 hot-press watercolor paper using
drawing pencils, ink, and watercolor.
MANUFACTURED IN CHINA
10 9 8 7 6 5 4 3 2 1
First Edition

Born and Bred in the Great Depression

by
JONAH WINTER

Illustrated by
KIMBERLY BULCKEN ROOT

schwartz & wade books · new york

Where you grew up, on the edge of town,
next to the tracks,
you could hear the trains going by
at night.

East Texas,
the 1930s—
the Great Depression.

In that tiny white frame house,
there were ten of you—
eight kids
and your parents—in four small rooms.

You slept at the foot of one bed
because there were only two beds
and you were the youngest.
You had to read by kerosene lanterns
because you couldn't afford electricity.

You got your water from a well
because there was no indoor plumbing.
There were no toilets,
so you had to use an outhouse.

I know, because you've told me, Dad.
This was the world you grew up in.

There weren't any jobs, or not many,
and sometimes your dad, Grandpa Winter, couldn't find work.
He'd make the slow walk home empty-handed,
past the storefronts,
over the bridge,
all the way to the edge of town

where the poorest people lived.
Waiting for him there
were nine mouths to feed
with no money.

Some mornings, at the lumberyard
where Grandpa sometimes worked,
he had to run a footrace against other men like him.
If he won, that meant he got to work that day.
That meant he'd won the right to sweat

in the hot Texas sun, painting railroad ties with tar,
hoisting them up when they were dry,
for ten cents an hour.
Low-paying work was better than no work at all.

During those years,
you spent your summers daydreaming,
exploring the woods behind your house.

I wonder what you dreamed about.
Were you dreaming
of a different world?

With no money
for new shoes,
your feet got tough as leather
walking barefoot down the gravel roads,

walking on the hot rails
day after day—that's what you've said.
But you've also said
you never went hungry.

There were vegetables
and fruit from the garden—
corn and okra, tomatoes, watermelons,
peas and potatoes and collard greens.

What you couldn't eat right away,
your mom would store in Mason jars—
apples and peaches and pears,
sealed until the winter.

And there were always eggs,
and there was often chicken—
everyone's favorite—
fried up in a cast-iron skillet.

How hard Granny Winter must have worked,
feeding so many people,
especially with you and David
and Harry and Lew
and Ada and Oleta
all too young to help.

The way you describe her, Granny Winter
did everything—cooking, cleaning,
gardening, milking.

But even as strong and as tough as she was,
she went a little crazy sometimes.
You've said that she was so afraid of storms,

she'd make you all go down in the storm cellar,
where she'd cry and pray,
wailing,
"Oh Lord, we're all gonna die!"

She wasn't scared of much else, though.
Like the time a bull
wandered into your pasture through an open gate—
she just grabbed it by its horns and led it out.

Sometimes it's hard to believe
this world was even real.
Maybe I've remembered it wrong.

Did Grandpa Winter really know a hermit
who lived in the woods
and ate beans from a jar?

Did Granny Winter really have to fire up the
    wood-burning stove
every day, even in the summer,
to heat up water
to wash clothes on a washboard?

Did you really see hoboes
leave little markings
right on your mailbox—
a code

to let other hoboes know
that this house was friendly?
Granny Winter gave them mashed-bean sandwiches
and leftover chicken

in exchange for their chopping wood.
And while they chopped,
your father would listen to their stories,
ask them where they'd been.

Where were they headed,
sleeping in boxcars,
a thousand miles away from home?

Riding the rails from one strange town
to the next,
no money, no family,
how did they survive?

On the radio, you'd hear what life was like
in those northern cities, far away,
where people who'd lost their homes
had to move into shacks made of cardboard,

side by side with other shacks,
makeshift towns in public parks,
Hoovervilles, you called them,
named after President Herbert Hoover,

whom many blamed
for the Great Depression.
"I don't know what caused it," you've said.
"All I know is that, poor as we were, my folks

never took one dime from the government."
Maybe they should have.
Maybe that would have made life easier for you.
But somehow, Dad, you survived.

And there were things that made life bearable:
A trip with your father to the icehouse,
riding up front in his old Model T,
to pick up a block of ice.

At Christmastime, you might not have gotten
many toys,

but it was magical to watch
the trains pass by,
to see the blue lights
twinkling in the windows of the dining car.

And it was a good day
if you got to play chess
with your dad

or listen to him play the banjo on the porch
in his special style,
two fingers gone
from a lumber mill accident.

You tell me
he read a library book every night,
in that dim light from the kerosene lamps,
after the cares of the day were done. . . .

When I think of the Great Depression,
I picture a whole country
of people tough as Grandpa and Granny Winter,
not giving up, even when

it seemed like there was nothing left to lose—
waiting out a storm that seemed like
it would never end
and then finally waking
to the blue skies of better days.

And I see you, Dad,
in your little overalls,
listening to the trains,
walking through the woods,

learning to love those things
that didn't cost a single penny.

Ada, Dad, and Granny Winter, circa 1937.

David, Ada, Oleta, Harry, and Lew, circa 1936.

Lew, David, and Dad, circa 1939.

Granny and Grandpa Winter, circa 1951.